Two
animal stories

The horse and the donkey
page 2

The car and the bullock cart
page 13

Nelson

The horse and the donkey

A long time ago, there was a farmer.
He had a big brown horse and
he had a small grey donkey.
The horse and the donkey helped him
on his farm.

Every week the farmer
went to market.
He put four sacks of apples on
the back of the poor grey donkey.
The poor donkey had to carry
the sacks to the market.

Each week as they went along
the dusty road to the market
the horse said to the donkey,
"I am such a big horse.
Don't you wish you were like me?"

"No, I don't," said the poor donkey.
"But I wish you would help me
carry these sacks to the market.
They are very heavy and
I am very tired."

"No," said the horse.

"I don't want to help you.

I won't carry sacks like a donkey."

So the poor donkey walked on

down the long dusty road.

When they came to the town
all the people said,
"Look at that big horse."
The horse heard them and
held his head up.
"I am the best horse in the land,"
he said.

When the people saw the poor
grey donkey they said,
"Look at that poor donkey.
He has too many sacks on his back.
Why can't the horse help him?"
The farmer heard the people.

He said to the horse,

"You must help the donkey.

You must carry two sacks of apples

to the market."

"Not me," said the horse.

"I won't carry sacks like a donkey."

9

One day the donkey had to stop.
He was so tired that he fell down
in the dusty road.
He could not get up again.
"What shall I do now?"
said the farmer.
"How shall I get my apples to market?"

Then he looked at the horse.

"You must carry the apples," he said.

"Oh no," said the horse.

"I can't do that."

"Oh yes, you can," said the farmer.

"You can carry all the sacks and
you can carry the donkey as well."

So the farmer put all the sacks of
apples on the back of the horse.
He put the donkey on the back
of the horse.
Then he sat himself on the back
of the horse.
And off they went down the long
dusty road to the market.

The car and
the bullock cart

There was once a man who had
a new red car.
He liked driving his new car.
"My car goes very fast," he said.
"I will have a race."

But who was there to race with?
There wasn't another car and
there wasn't a bus and
there wasn't a train.
There were only two bullocks
pulling a cart.
The driver of the cart was asleep.

"We will race your new red car,"
said the bullocks.
"Ha. Ha. Ha," said the man.
"You can't go as fast as my new car
and your driver is asleep."
"We can win the race,"
said the bullocks.

"All right," said the man.

"I will race you. Let's go."

So *zoom* went the car down the road.

And *clip clop* went the bullocks

down the road.

Zoom went the car down the road.
Then the man wanted
a drink of water.
"The bullocks can't catch up
with me," he said.
He stopped the car to get
a drink of water.
But *clip clop* went the bullocks
down the road.

17

Zoom went the car down the road.

Then the man felt hungry.

"The bullocks can't catch up
with me," he said.

He stopped the car to get
some food.

But *clip clop* went the bullocks
down the road.

Zoom went the car down the road.
Then the man felt tired.
"The bullocks can't catch up
with me," he said.
He stopped the car under a tree and
went to sleep.
But *clip clop* went the bullocks
down the road.

The bullocks walked on and on
clip clop down the road.
They walked on past the car and
they walked on past the man.
They walked down the road until
they saw the end of the race.

All the children were waiting
to see who won the race.
"Come on, bullocks,"
said the children.
"You will win the race."
And the bullocks walked across
the line, *clip clop, clip clop*.

The man woke up and saw
the sun was going down.
"I must hurry if I want
to win the race," he said.
He got in the car and
zoom it went down the road.
But the man was too late.
The bullocks had won
the race already.

"I went to sleep," the man said
to the bullocks.
"That is why you won the race."
"Our driver is asleep all the time,"
said the bullocks.
"We can win a race without a driver."

So the man got in his car and
went back down the road, *zoom*.
The bullocks went back down
the road *clip clop* and
the driver of the bullock cart
was still fast asleep.
He never knew the bullocks had
been in a race and won.
But they had.